The Hurry-Up Exit from Egypt

written by Gary Bower | illustrated by Barbara Chotiner

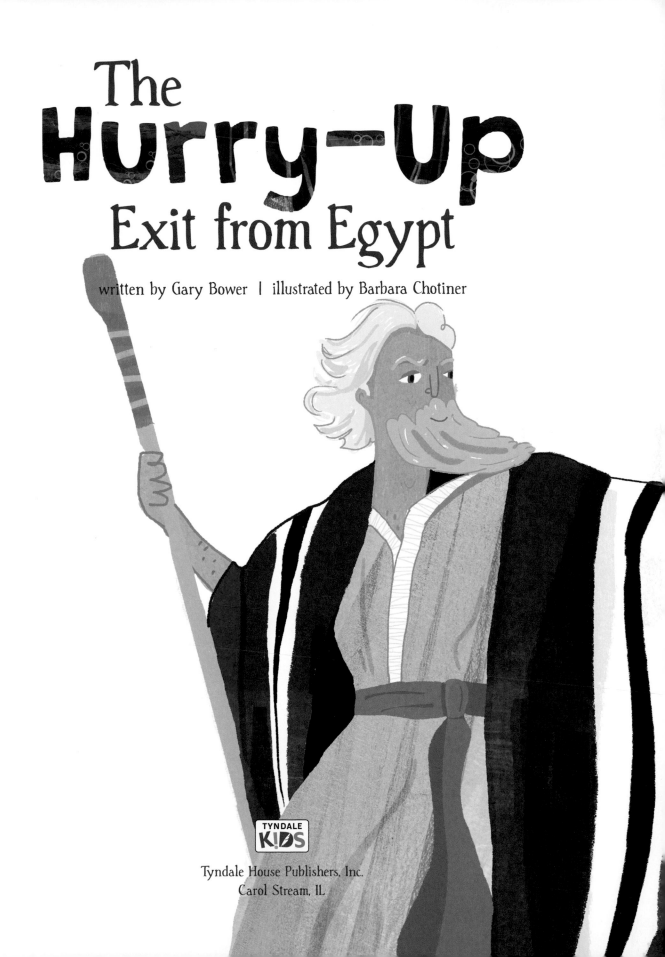

TYNDALE KIDS

Tyndale House Publishers, Inc.
Carol Stream, IL

To Inga, Destry, Miriam, and Judah

Visit Tyndale's website for kids at www.tyndale.com/kids.

Visit Gary Bower online at www.bowerarts.com.

TYNDALE is a registered trademark of Tyndale House Publishers, Inc. The Tyndale Kids logo is a trademark of Tyndale House Publishers, Inc.

The Hurry-Up Exit from Egypt

Designed by Jacqueline L. Nuñez

Edited by Sarah Rubio

Scripture quotations are taken from the *Holy Bible*, New Living Translation, copyright © 1996, 2004, 2015 by Tyndale House Foundation. Used by permission of Tyndale House Publishers, Inc., Carol Stream, Illinois 60188. All rights reserved.

For manufacturing information regarding this product, please call 1-800-323-9400.

For information about special discounts for bulk purchases, please contact Tyndale House Publishers at csresponse@tyndale.com or call 800-323-9400.

Library of Congress Cataloging-in-Publication Data
Names: Bower, Gary, date, author.
Title: The hurry-up exit from Egypt / Gary Bower.
Description: Carol Stream, Illinois : Tyndale House Publishers, [2017]
  | Series: The faith that God built | Audience: Ages 4–7. | Audience: K to
  grade 3.
Identifiers: LCCN 2016010623 | ISBN 9781496417459 (hc)
Subjects: LCSH: Moses (Biblical leader)--Juvenile literature. | Bible.
  Exodus--Juvenile literature. | Exodus, The--Juvenile literature. |
  Jews--History--To 1200 B.C.--Juvenile literature. | Egypt--History--To 332
  B.C.--Juvenile literature.
Classification: LCC BS580.M6 B69 2017 | DDC 222.1209505--dc23 LC record available at https://lccn.loc.gov/2016010623

Printed in China

23	22	21	20	19	18	17
7	6	5	4	3	2	1

This is **the exit from Egypt.**

These are **the feet that were frantic and fleet** on **the hurry-up exit from Egypt.**

3

These are **the Israelites thrown in a fit,**
panicking, scampering lickety-split
On scurrying **feet that were frantic and
fleet** on **the hurry-up exit from Egypt.**

These are **King Pharaoh's frightening forces**—drivers on chariots, riders on horses—

Chasing **the Israelites thrown in a fit,**
panicking, scampering lickety-split

8

On scurrying **feet that were frantic and fleet** on **the hurry-up exit from Egypt.**

This is **the sea that made them all cry,**
"We're trapped here like rats, and we're all gonna die!"

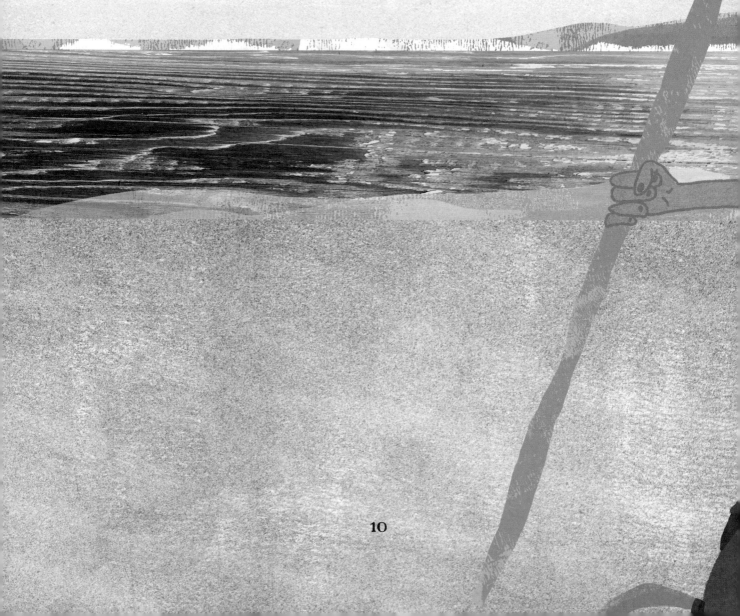

While fleeing **King Pharaoh's frightening forces**—drivers on chariots, riders on horses—

Chasing **the Israelites thrown in a fit,**
panicking, scampering lickety-split

On scurrying **feet that were frantic and fleet** on **the hurry-up exit from Egypt.**

13

This is **old Moses raising his rod** and parting the waves by the power of God,
Who blew back **the sea that made them all cry,** "We're trapped here like rats, and we're all gonna die!"

15

While fleeing **King Pharaoh's frightening forces**—drivers on chariots, riders on horses—
Chasing **the Israelites thrown in a fit,** panicking, scampering lickety-split
On scurrying **feet that were frantic and fleet** on **the hurry-up exit from Egypt.**

This is **their pathway, an eye-popping sight,** with water heaped high
on the left and the right,
After **old Moses had lifted his rod** and
parted the waves by the power of God,

19

Who blew back **the sea that made them all cry,** "We're trapped here like rats, and we're all gonna die!" While fleeing **King Pharaoh's frightening forces**—drivers on chariots, riders on horses—

Chasing **the Israelites thrown in a fit,** panicking, scampering lickety-split On scurrying **feet that were frantic and fleet** on **the hurry-up exit from Egypt.**

These are **the chariots, hot on their heels,** with hobbly, wobbly, wiggly wheels,

Pursuing **their pathway, an eye-popping sight,** with water heaped high on the left and the right,

After **old Moses had lifted his rod**
and parted the waves by the power of God,
Who blew back **the sea that made
them all cry,** "We're trapped here like rats,
and we're all gonna die!"

While fleeing **King Pharaoh's frightening forces**—drivers on chariots, riders on horses— Chasing **the Israelites thrown in a fit,** panicking, scampering lickety-split On scurrying **feet that were frantic and fleet** on **the hurry-up exit from Egypt.**

25

This is **the Book that tells of the day** God stopped their pursuers and swept them away,

After **the chariots, hot on their heels,** with hobbly, wobbly, wiggly wheels,

Pursuing **their pathway, an eye–popping sight**, with water heaped high on the left and the right,
After **old Moses had lifted his rod** and parted the waves by the power of God,
Who blew back **the sea that made them all cry**, "We're trapped here like rats, and we're all gonna die!"

While fleeing **King Pharaoh's frightening forces**—drivers on chariots, riders on horses—
Chasing **the Israelites thrown in a fit,** panicking, scampering lickety-split
On scurrying **feet that were frantic and fleet** on **the hurry-up exit from Egypt.**

For the whole story,
see Exodus 12–14.

The Lord is my strength
and my song; he has
given me victory.
EXODUS 15:2